THE COLOR OF HORSES

DR. BEN K. GREEN

THE COLOR OF HORSES

The Scientific and Authoritative Identification
of the Color of the Horse

With paintings by Darol Dickinson

NORTHLAND PRESS

CONTENTS

DR. BEN K. GREEN

INSIGHT INTO HORSE COLOR

I FIRST HEARD the color of horses discussed and began to know that some people preferred different colors of horses for different reasons when I was washing buggy wheels at the livery stable the year before I was old enough to go to public school. Sometimes I would give those buggy wheels an extra good washing if there were a discussion going on among the men in the livery stable about the color of horses. I learned at a tender age that the teams that were matched in color and size were more highly prized by their owners than teams made up of different colored horses.

Old horsemen all seem to have their own choice of color. I remember a traveling salesman, who was referred to as a drummer in those days, that rode the train to Cumby and then hired a team and hack to call on his various customers around the trade territory. This was a fancy-dressed fellow who was a loud talker and always made a point that he would rather have a solid bay team because they had more endurance. Then I heard other colors discussed and various reasons and excuses given for liking and disliking them.

As a small boy, so far as I was concerned, walking was all took up when I was born. I saddled a horse after breakfast and unsaddled before I went to bed the first twenty-five to thirty years of my life and decided early that if color had anything to do with stamina, intelligence or soundness, I had better learn about it. I heard old cowboys brag especially about the many good qualities of dun and buckskin horses. However, I had begun to notice by the time I was a teenage boy that you rarely saw horses of fine breeding that were of dun color.

By the time I was in the fourth and fifth grade in school, I was trading a good many horses. Occasionally somebody would ask me to try to find them a horse of a particular color which in those days was not hard to do since there were lots of horses. In the early part of my horse experience dapple greys and various shades of chestnut horses were harder to find than the general run of bays and browns. There were few solid black horses, but there was a demand

1

for the color. However, I frequently heard the complaint that black horses "sunburned" too bad in the summertime, and their color was too hard to keep.

Blacksmiths told me that white feet were worse to split and were softer to cut and shape than dark-colored feet. I soon began to know that a horse of any color that had one or more white feet would have to be kept shod in order to be able to stand constant use. When I was about eighteen years old, there was a great fad on for spotted horses, and I traded around until I came up with some good, young spotted horses of various color patterns and average ranch size and began to use them hard. I learned that the white foot story was still true and began to notice that the white hide of a spotted horse if under the saddle or the cinch was quicker to skin and scald from sweat and heat than the dark hide of the same horse. I also began to know from observing my horses and those belonging to other riders that blistery faces and irritated eyes were common to bald-faced horses in cases where the white extended out over the eyes. White hair has no refraction of light qualities and does not afford white skin under it any protection, and the absorption of extreme heat reflects and irritates white hide, whereas the dark hair of a dark hide refracts the sun rays and deflects those damaging effects to the extent that no harm is done to the more durable dark hide.

Dun, buckskin and grulla horses have long been described by early-day cowboys as being the toughest horses the West ever had. I had heard this conversation for a good while. During my teenage years and early twenties I rode long hours in rough country and was extremely hard on horses, and it took several to keep me mounted. I decided that if there were anything to this toughness of the native colors dun, buckskin and grulla that it was about time I tried them out. In the course of about three months I bought and traded for three young dun geldings, two good-bodied buckskin mares and two grullas, a mare and a gelding. These horses ranged in age from four to eight years, and in my opinion these are the best years for hard use in a horse's lifetime. I was careful to get horses with good feet and legs and well-balanced bodies that should stay sound regardless of color.

I was working a good many feedlot cattle that required me to be mounted on quick horses that could stay under me day in and day out. At this particular time I was buying and gathering lots of mules from over a wide scope of country for resale. During the fall, winter and spring, I learned how these coat colors got their reputations for being tough. All seven head stayed sound in spite of hard riding, but here was the answer to their toughness. These colors belong to horses of native, western breeding that have very little hot blood infused into them and self preservation and survival is much more instinctive than in the hotter breeds of horses that have been bred for performance. There was very little fretting nor the unnecessary or excessive use of energy in these colors of horses. The reasons they were considered tough is because the rider worked a little harder at getting them to do, and they stopped a little short before they ran out of wind or were completely used up. It might be said, with few exceptions, that horses with these colors always take better care of themselves and are less responsive to the demands of the rider and less affected by the length of the workday, and their reputation for toughness results from their instinct for self-preservation and survival.

Horsemen that were particularly fond of chestnut and sorrel horses would argue that they had more sense or that they were faster or possibly had more action than horses of other colors. I began to notice some chestnut horses were good performers in cutting and roping and also in sports events such as polo and open jumping. So I decided I needed some chestnut horses. The fact of the matter is there weren't many horses tough enough to stand young cowboys in their late teens and early twenties. So these rugged cowhands were always hunting for a better horse. I was quick to detect the difference in the performance ability of chestnut and sorrel horses as compared to horses of other colors. The sorrels and chestnuts that I came in contact with had an infusion of some percentage of Thoroughbred blood which gave them more action and more speed. However, they were tender mouthed, and it took a little better horsemanship to keep from ruining their mouths and performance ability. It was also evident that the darker shades had better feet, better reflective qualities in the hair around their eyes and were less subject to scalding and chafing by saddles and cinches. The light shades of chestnut and sorrel had less darkness in their feet and were more trouble to keep shod.

Most palomino horses had amber-colored eyes, and if there were no white markings in their face, their eyes wouldn't get sore and run. But their skin was less durable than the darker-colored horses.

In my growing-up years I saw a good many grey horses at hard ranch work and being driven by the public to various kinds of carriages and delivery wagons. Even though the color of a grey horse gets lighter as it grows older, the skin will be exceptionally tough and withstand the use of harness and saddle with a minimum amount of damage.

Consistently, bay, whether occurring in hot-blooded horses or native, western-bred horses, has always been the most serviceable, and without exception could stand much heat and hard use with very little discoloration from the sun. From my experience in all cases, bay, in its various shades, is the most serviceable color worn by a horse.

I have also ridden, driven and worked a few black horses throughout my lifetime. Well kept, it is a beautiful color, and the hide of black horses is consistently good, but the absorption of light and heat causes black horses to begin to "sunburn" (fade) in hotter climates. When that happens, they do not retain from one season to the next the black color that they display when they have a fresh coat of hair on them. Otherwise a black horse is very desirable in usefulness and appearance.

In favorable climates lighter hides do not make as much difference in the usefulness of a horse. Extremely hot climates bear out and prove the difference and desirability of dark-hided horses. In some of the hottest regions of the world where the soil is very sandy and carries a high percentage of a glass-like substance which has a high reflective quality, the term "sand scald" is used to refer to the reaction of horses' hides that cannot stand the heat from the sun and the reflected heat from the sand. There is a region in South Texas and along the Rio Grande border in Mexico where "sand scald" is a major problem in horses. The darkest colors with the least possible white markings suffer very little, if any, "sand scald" damage, whereas patches of hide on light chestnuts, light sorrels, palominos and the white markings on any other color of horse are subject to summer blistering from the reflective heat of the sand. There is another such region in South America where it seems that a persistent hot wind causes this condition to be considerably worse. The sand-burned areas of a horse split and crack and bleed much more severely because of the drying effect from the hot winds. In the Syrian desert of the Middle East, light-colored horses or horses with white markings are virtually unknown because of the hundreds of years that the Arabs of that area have culled their breeding stock of any light-hided horses. However, when one does appear in any of the lighter shades, the sun and sand scald the skin, burning into the unprotected flesh and causing more severe sores and scars than the other two "sand scald" regions of the world that I know of. It is interesting to note that these separate areas are very nearly the same distance from the equator. There may be other parts of the world which have the same conditions, but not to my personal knowledge.

I began to notice that teamsters doing heavy public hauling and dirt contracting always preferred dark-hided horses. Grey horses were popular with teamsters, and for the most part, the color came from Percheron draft blood. A grey horse always has a heavy, black hide and the so-called top color of the horse would not make any difference in his service.

As a young man buying horses and mules in almost every part of the United States, and on several occasions going to foreign countries to buy and import registered breeding horses, I learned that there were preferences for certain colors in different countries, such as the English breeds, the Cleveland Bay and the Suffolk Punch (which is supposed to be chestnut). However, the Cleveland Bay had many of the throwbacks of black horses, and the Suffolk Punch varied through the seven shades of chestnut with occasional red roans appearing even though this color had been culled for many years. Dapple grey was the choice color for Percheron horses in France. However, there were many blacks that were bred out of grey and of course, the Percheron breed had other colors too.

I ran horses on the desert in the Middle East with the Arabs, and contrary to public opinion there was only a small percentage of grey Arabian horses. Most of the Arabian horses were solid shades of bay and brown with black points and black manes and tails. There were always some chestnuts, and even some grullas occasionally showed up in desert horses. However, from my observation of Arabians, dun and buckskin were not Arabian colors. I never saw a palomino or any other dilute color on the desert. The old chieftains told me that they originally prized the grey horses because mixed with a band of horses of other colors, they created a camouflage appearance on the desert and were harder to see at a distance.

I had tried to breed different colors in my own band of brood mares. Never did I have more than seventy percent success regardless of which solid colors I bred together. In so-called book research I read about genetics and what produced grey horses and horses of other colors. None of it ever proved out in a breeding program, and I wondered if the genetic geniuses who wrote such books were actually horse breeders or were breeding them on paper and in theory only. It was common knowledge among horsemen that the most prepotent of studs could not mark the color of his offspring where he was bred to a mare of equal breeding but of different color.

As the machine age developed, I watched the population of horses dwindle and was aware of the disappearance of some colors in horses. There were changes in the percentages of colors that were present in the horses that were being bred but not kept entirely for hard useful purposes. In 1942 I established a laboratory in my practice at Fort Stockton, Texas, in the Trans Pecos Region which was the last stronghold for big bands of range, brood mares. The horse was still being used extensively in ranch operations in a country that would never become entirely taken over by the machine age. This was a big horse country. Horses were cheap at the time, and there was an array of colors that could not have been found anywhere else in North America. Since nothing I had ever read in genetics would directly produce a high percentage of an intended color, I decided to do research on the hair and hide of horses to determine what made color.

My first crude attempts to extract color from hair were complete failures, and after about three months of trying without any success, I decided to find a technician who would help me. I knew a Mr. Busche in New York City, who was an outstanding analytical chemist and laboratory technician. We had worked together on botanical projects in the past, and I decided it was time he learned something about the color of horses. I went to New York to visit with him, and after we had our howdys and light conversation, I propositioned him on the matter of horse color. After a long evening of discussion he consented to work with me in order that we might arrive at some method of extracting pigment from horsehair and hide. Both of us knew it was going to be a painstaking process and highly unprofitable. I spent about a week in the laboratory with him, learning the techniques that we would use in our attempts to extract pigment from hair and hide. We agreed for me to send him samples of hair to work on, and we would exchange ideas and results by correspondence and telephone until we found the laboratory process that would extract pigment or until I gave up the project, which Busche said wasn't likely.

In the beginning I clipped hair from various colors of horses with a pair of curved scissors, and we endeavored to extract a pigment from this hair. I began to be able to get some color out of the hair at my laboratory, but by the time the hair was shipped to New York, with the change of temperature from a live horse to an envelope together with atmospheric and light changes, it would not yield anything for Busche even though he used the same process I might be using at the same time.

One day I was called to sew up a horse that had been badly cut on a barbed wire fence when a band of horses had been buzzed by an airplane from a nearby air training field. Much of the hide from the neck, breast and forearm of this dark chestnut horse was dangling, and in spite of my best surgical efforts, there was a small piece of hide that had to be cut off. I removed this small piece of hide, threw it in the dirt and finished attending to the horse's wound. I got in my car and was halfway back to town when I realized how stupid a man could get when he is searching for something. I turned around and went back to the corral and found the small piece of hide and washed it off in a water trough. I went directly to my laboratory and started doing a dermis dissection. I called Busche in New York, and he told me how he thought pigment might be extracted from the tissue of the horse's hide. By midnight I had about two drops of amber fluid which was the first time that we had been able to extract pigment in its fluid form.

made slides from it. By using the various laboratory stains on it I detected that the pigment was a round globule substance that later proved to be a protein. These small round objects were identifiable only under the strongest focus that I had in my good laboratory microscope.

During the process of pigment extraction, I determined that horsehair is hollow, that the pigment is inside the shaft of the hair and that the walls of the hair itself are clear. I started the process by placing the hair on a slide under the strongest focus of my microscope, and I began to discover pattern arrangements of these microscopic, round, amber globules. It was in the third year of research that I began to understand that it is the arrangement pattern of the pigment in the shaft of the hair and the density of pigment that refracts the light and reflects the color that is identified by the human eye as being bay, chestnut or any other color.

This finding caused me to start splitting hairs under the microscope in order to further determine the true arrangement of each pigment pattern of different colors and shades of colors. I also began to wonder about highlights that appeared on a well-kept horse's coat. I would take from twenty to as many as sixty hair samples from the different areas of a hide and paste them down with adhesive under the microscope and split them with an electric blade. This enabled me to make microscopic photographs of the true pattern arrangement of the pigment. After splitting some four thousand hairs during my years of research, I have excellent proof in my records as to the density or lack of density and the arrangement of the amber pigment particles that refract the light and reflect various colors and shades.

Under microscopic observation it can be determined that there are three active sections of a hair that serve a specific purpose in the arrangement of the pigment globules. That arrangement causes certain patterns that affect the refraction of light. The first section of the hair is the root. The root of the hair is slightly flared and as the skin moves in its various motions, this flared root gathers and sucks up the microscopic particles of pigment.

The second section of the hair is an enlargement above the root that microscopically is a drumlike section larger than the root and larger than the extending shaft of the hair. It is this drumlike section called a follicle, and the manner in which the pigment is transmitted from the follicle, that determines its pattern of arrangement in the shaft of the hair. The microscopic pigment particles migrate through the follicle and up through the shaft of the hair by their own electrons. This explains the presence of the different patterns formed by the same color pigmentation, and it is the difference in the density and the lack of density in the various patterns that refract light to reflect the different known colors and the various shades within the colors of a horse.

The third section is the shaft of the hair that extends out of the hide above the follicle, and it makes the body coat of the horse, serves the overall purpose of protecting the horse and holds the permanent pigment arrangement.

Each color treated in this book will show the pigment arrangement refraction pattern that causes a certain color or shade of a color.

In the days of my research I was practicing in an area of two hundred miles every direction from my home-office in Fort Stockton, Texas, where lots of horses and hides and different colors were easy to come by. This research extended over a period of five years from 1942 to 1947. I occasionally worked on the extraction of pigment as late as 1950 if a hide of unusual color happened to show up. This research was done for the sole reason of satisfying my own curiosity about the coloring of horses. At that time I had not the slightest idea of ever putting my research into book form, but because Busche made such elaborate notes on what he did and mailed them to me, I felt that I should follow his example. So I made very explicit notes on each hide and extract, wrote them up, filed them with my other office records, and sent him a copy

During this same period of time I established a set of breeding records on three hundred and fifty mares. Over a period of ten years, seventy-six different studs were used on these various bands of mares. These bands of mares and studs were on open range fenced pastures and were pasture bred with no handling or human interference with their breeding habits. They produced more than an eighty percent foal crop over a period of ten years.

Two bands of mares were of native mustang stock, mostly bays with some shades of dun and buckskin color. They were being bred by two Arabian stallions, one solid bay and the

11

other dark chestnut. Four bands of mares were principally of Thoroughbred breeding, and a fifth band was also of Thoroughbred breeding but with a strong infusion of Arabian blood. Seventy percent of these five bands were of some shade of bay or brown and the remaining percentage some shade of chestnut. These mares were being bred to registered Thoroughbred stallions that were either bay, brown or chestnut. One band of mares was mostly black and had backgrounds of Percheron blood with three Thoroughbred crosses on them and were bred to a dark bay Thoroughbred stallion. Another band of mares were grade Morgan mares, mostly bays and browns, but almost pure Morgan breeding, and were bred to a registered liver chestnut Morgan stallion. The other two remaining bands of eleven mares were the average run of light-boned, western-bred horses of common ranch type and were being bred to one black American Quarter Horse and one sorrel American Quarter Horse. When a mare or stud needed replacing, the same color was used.

It is true that bay bred to bay will produce a large percentage of bay foals, and it does hold true that breeding like colors will produce a high percentage of foals of the same color, but in no case in the records of these mares for ten years could it ever be said that you can predict the color of a foal. I would point out that the purest and darkest of the bays produced a noticeable number (thirty percent) of blacks and browns. Chestnut, being a recessive color, was produced to some extent in all bands of mares regardless of their colors or the colors of the sires. In other words, there were as many chestnuts produced from solid-colored sires and dams (not chestnut) as there were from those matings involving one chestnut parent.

The statement has been made in literature since man began to write about horses that grey foals must have one grey ancestor. In the black mares with the one-quarter to one-eighth Percheron background being bred to a dark bay Thoroughbred stallion, there were two beautiful grey colts the third year that I kept records. They were born black and changed to steel grey by the time they were two-year-olds and dapple grey by the time they were four. In another band of mares, there was a bright chestnut mare with no white markings that produced five red roan foals in seven years. Light chestnut sires and dams crossbred to the native buckskin color produced forty percent of their entire foal number in dilutes known as palominos.

In view of my laboratory findings and the foals produced by these mares over a period of ten years, it is not possible for me to agree with the chapter on color in Tesio's book, *Breeding the Race Horse,* published in 1958, or with any writer before or since who has not through laboratory research extracted the pigmentation from the hair and hide of a horse. The most exhaustive research of any kind should be substantiated by actual practice, such as the breeding of large numbers of horses and the observation of their offspring through a period of several years.

I have never resorted to the research of written pedigrees described by human beings of all nationalities who might have varied opinions and ways of describing color that could easily be confusing. I am referring to the difference between bay or brown or what shade would be considered light or dark and the many other varying judgments and analyses arrived at by the human eye to determine any genetical factors pertaining to color. Written pedigrees and written subject matter by horsemen of other ages is subject to as much error as the judgment and opinion of the horseman of this age. The only worthwhile research pertaining to the color of a horse should be obtained by the extraction of pigment from the hair, hide, mane and tail of a horse and the microscopic examination of the arrangement of the pigment bodies in the shaft of the hair. This method should be free from any suspicion of incorrect description of colors as identified by different human eyes.

For more than two hundred years scientists and especially geneticists have listened to and practiced the theories of Mendel, the great botanist of his time who established Mendel's Law in the hybrid crossing of peas. It is true, and I am more than willing to concede, that Mendel's Law has been a great governing factor and contribution to the improvement of plant varieties by agricultural and plant scientists. However, scientists who do their research from the manuscripts and printed matter of others, I term reading scientists. Those people have gone far amiss in their attempts to apply Mendel's Law to animal life and especially to domestic animal life. From research actually done on the horse, I cannot agree with the writings and conclusions

13

drawn by old writers who have reached their suppositions and conclusions by applying Mendel's Law to animal life.

The strongest evidence against applying Mendel's Law to animal life is clearly shown by a fact which has been proven many times. In the case of sires and dams of equal breeding, the sire marks his dominant characteristics on the female offspring, and the dam marks her dominant characteristics on the male offspring. This pattern is further borne out in the explicit records of racing breeds where sires become known as the sires of dams that produce winners, and the dams become known for producing male offspring that are dominated by her characteristics, which in effect is the transposition from her sire to her male offspring. These facts are proven by hundreds of written records especially in the racing breeds of horses, and they clearly show that Mendel's Law cannot be applied in the breeding of horses. There are many other exceptions in the production of domestic meat animals and dairy cattle that defy the principle of Mendel's Law.

The writers of the early nineteenth century who relied on Mendel's theory and those of the twentieth century who have had scientific opportunities to do true research on the horse have settled for the conclusions and old expressions of the writers of another century. In doing this they have fallen far short of their goals and responsibilities to the present-day horse breeder.

The facts written and illustrated in this book are not conclusions drawn from other inadequate, secondary sources but have been gained by extensive, time-consuming, exhaustive research on many horses of all breeds. During this period of extensive research I have extracted the pigment from the hair and hide of one hundred and thirty-five horses. The findings of this basic laboratory research are the basis for this book.

Hair and Hide

THE CONDITION OF THE HAIR AND HIDE OF A HORSE is the best barometer of its general health and can be determined at a glance by the amateur or professional horseman. The exception to the rule is that a horse staying outside during winter weather will have longer hair and less sheen than in other seasons of the year, and will naturally differ in appearance from a horse kept inside and properly groomed.

The hide of a horse has very fine oil glands that secrete the necessary oils to keep the hide pliable and resistant to weather and other abuse. These oil glands are so small they can only be identified under a microscope.

These same oils protect and give gloss to the shafts of hair extending all the way to their points. In the refraction of light from the hair, the sheen and the gloss show when a horse is in its healthiest condition and is properly groomed. For a horse to be in excellent condition, the hide must be pliable when felt by the hand and the oil glands' secretions must be sufficient to cause the hair to have a sheen and possess good light refraction qualities. A fat horse without this general hide and hair condition is not necessarily a healthy horse.

The condition of the hair is dependent on the outside oil and there is no substance that secretes through the hair, meaning that the only way to cause "bloom" on a horse is to brush and gently rub the hair the same direction as it grows. The rubbing can be done with the palm of your hand or a soft finished cloth. Blanketing a horse causes the oils to be more abundant in the same manner as the gentle rubbing process. Any of the so-called hair conditioners that are used to give a horse "bloom" are of little value and short duration.

PIGMENTATION OF THE HAIR

HAIR IS FORMED FROM A PROTEIN called keratin, and the walls of the shaft of the hair are clear. They contain no melanin pigment. A horse's hide consists of sixteen layers of dermis tissue. Even though the top three layers of dermis tissue are well pigmented, there is no pigment available to be transmitted to the shaft of the hair. The pigment that colors the hair of a horse is produced by pigment glands that are housed in the next four layers of dermis tissue. These pigment bodies are microscopic in size. The other nine layers of dermis tissue contain the serum and blood that separate the upper part of the hide from the flesh.

Pigment in the hide, which is secreted by fine glands, is picked up by the roots of the hair

15

and it migrates by its own electrons into the follicle which is a barrel-like enlargement above the roots but beneath the shaft of the hair. The follicle is housed in the third layer of the dermis tissue in the hide of a horse. From this follicle the shaft continues to grow and tapers to the end of the hair. When the pigment forces itself through the opening at the top of the follicle into the shaft of the hair, it forms a pattern and migrates by its electrons to the extreme tip of the hair. The pattern that is formed as it leaves the follicle refracts light and reflects color according to the density or lack of density of pigment as it migrates into the shaft of the hair.

The root of a hair under microscopic examination is flared, and, since the hide is pliable, as an animal moves his hide the flared root of the hair moves also and creates a suction which introduces the pigment particles into the follicle. When hair is fully grown, and when its keratin walls are deteriorated by weather or by the presence of saddles, harness and other man-made contraptions, the root of the hair goes through an aging process. It shrinks and loses its flared-like shape. The follicle, having served its purpose, collapses, and because of the heat and sweat and gland secretions of the hide, ceases to be a barrel-like formation. When it shrinks, the hair loosens in the hide so that an animal may shed the deteriorated hair. After the shedding, the hair glands of the body produce new hair which repeats the same process. There are never any secretions from inside the hair, so when damage to the shaft of the hair is caused by weather, time, heat and pressure, the entrance of foreign matter dulls the pigment which results in fading, sunburn and discoloration.

In order to understand the reason that one pigment colors all horses, it is necessary to understand the pigment movement from the hide of a horse into the roots, up through the follicle and into the shaft. The pattern by which the pigment passes from the opening at the top of the follicle creates the pattern that refracts light in its different ways and reflects the color that we optically identify with a horse.

If the opening of the follicle is wide and pigment easily passes into the shaft of the hair in such abundance and intensity that no light is reflected from it, the color is black.

The arrangement that forms the other patterns as the pigment leaves the opening of the follicle and enters into the shaft of the hair determines what color and what shade of color a horse will optically appear to be to the observer. For example, the pattern for the color palomino, which is a dilute, shows that the opening of the follicle is drawn extremely small, and pigment is forced out by its electrons into a thin smear that coats the inside of the shaft of the hair.

SHADES OF COLOR

THERE IS AN EXTENSIVE ARRAY of shades of color, and a horse may have several shades of the same color distributed over various parts of the body. For instance, a bay horse might have a standard bay shoulder and middle and a mahogany rump; or a dark chestnut may have a mixed flax mane and tail and possibly a lighter neck than the rest of the body. These are cited as examples of variance of color.

This book, *The Color of Horses,* will not attempt to treat all the varying shades within a color. The colors and the shades of color set forth in this book are those that have been recognized by horsemen through the ages as the standard and appropriate describable shades within the various colors. It is not intended to imply that an individual horse of various undescribed shades is still not known as a bay, chestnut, or whatever color category that particular horse belongs to.

INTENSE COLORS

BAY

Dark Bay

Mahogany Bay

Standard Bay

Blood Bay

Light Bay

BROWN

Standard Brown

Seal Brown

BLACK

Coal Black

Raven Black

GREY

Two-year-old

Three- to four-year-old

Four- to seven-year-old

Ten years and older

DUN

I
NTENSE COLORS OF HORSES are described as such because of the abundance of pigment, and the darkness of hide. This group includes bay, black, brown, grey and dun. Horsemen have known since the horse became a useful domestic animal that the intense colors withstand more abuse from the trappings of man such as harness and saddles than any of the lesser colors. The only real objection to intense colors is that some of the pigment patterns are inclined to absorb heat and refract and absorb light, and those patterns fade some from intense heat and excessive secretions from the sweat glands.

The saline content of horse sweat drys the outside shaft of the hair wall and causes fine cracks running parallel with the shaft of the hair that can only be detected by the best microscopic lens. These cracks allow sweat to enter the hair shaft where the pigment is located. The saline content of these sweat secretions dulls the pigmentation. This dullness is often observed in summertime and hot climates in the colors black, brown, and dark bay. The fading of color in the regions of saddles, harness and other man-made contraptions is caused by sweat and pressure and is often referred to as "sunburn."

BAY

BAY IN ITS SEVERAL SHADES was among the first to be valued for its eye appeal, usefulness and durability. Bay is an intense color, and its different shades are common to all breeds of horses. References are made to the different shades of bay being described in the early literature as dark bay, mahogany bay, standard bay, blood bay, and light bay. The only truth that can be derived from these various expressions is that the horse being described by such terms would fall in the general classification of bay.

Bay does not bleach out from the rubbing of saddles, harness and the effects of sweat as much as do the darker colors, black and brown. This is because of the remarkable amount of refraction and reflection of light that is performed by the particular pigment pattern of this color and because the pigment deposits are uniform in pattern and slightly larger than the individual pigment deposits of any other color.

Each separate body of pigment throws out a fine needle in every direction to fuse the entire pattern together and to stabilize the pigment within the hair. The darker shades of bay appear darker because each pigment body is larger than the standard bay pattern, thereby shutting out more light and portraying the darker shades of bay.

All bay horses regardless of their shade, in their purest color should have black legs extending from just above the knee and hock to the hoof, and the hooves should also be black. The correct description of such horses is "bay with black points." The only exception to this rule is that in the lightest shade of bay, light bay, the body color occasionally is mingled into the points.

DARK BAY

DARK BAY IS A COLOR that is often confused with brown, and due to the loss of talent in horsemen of this age, horses are being registered and consistently described as dark bay or brown. Such a description is a gross admittance of ignorance about the color of a horse. Dark bay, it is true, has a brown appearance in its overall body color; however, the bay markings can be found in the flanks, underbelly and muzzle of the horse and generally the inside of the hind legs have a very reddish bay color. The darker shades on the horse have the same bay pigment pattern but a greater intensity of pigment in the hair. To the untrained eye, a brown horse could have the appearance of a bay over the back, shoulders and rump, but the brown would never have the true bay cast in the other parts of its coat. The dark bay also has the overall bayish cast in the sheen of the dark areas that would indicate it is dark bay instead of brown.

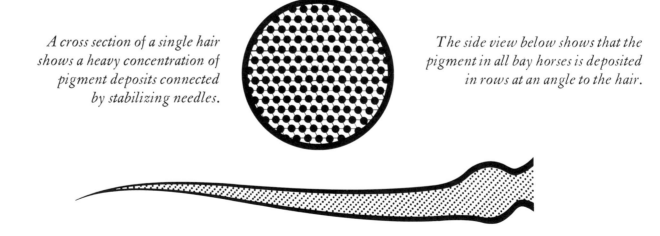

A cross section of a single hair shows a heavy concentration of pigment deposits connected by stabilizing needles.

The side view below shows that the pigment in all bay horses is deposited in rows at an angle to the hair.

DARK BAY: *Thoroughbred*

25

MAHOGANY BAY

A MAHOGANY BAY HORSE isn't nearly as dark as dark bay, however, it is dark over the rump and lesser regions along the back, ribs and shoulders. There is a combination of standard bay and dark bay pigment patterns distributed over the horse's body with standard bay showing in the flanks, neck and muzzle and highlights across the lower part of the hindquarters, shoulders and the inside of the legs. Darker shades make up the rest of the horse's body color.

This color is determined by alternating layers of dark bay and standard bay pigment patterns within each hair.

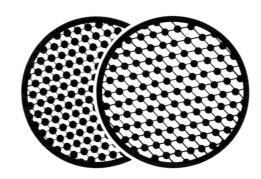

MAHOGANY BAY: *Thoroughbred*

27

STANDARD BAY

STANDARD BAY IS A UNIFORM COLOR of clear bay all over the body with the only dark hair being in the points which are from the middle joints of the legs to the hoof. A standard bay has a black mane and tail. Standard bay reflects light, absorbs less heat and possesses the same heavy dark hide as the darker colors. It rarely ever shows sunburn or any other type of discoloration. Because of all of its favorable qualities and the fact that it does not have the undesirable characteristics of the darker shades and a hide equally as durable, the color will long be the most useful of all shades of bay. It is one of the best, if not the best, colors to withstand abuse and maintain its true shade through all climatic conditions and hard work.

A less intense concentration of pigment deposits allows a greater refraction of light. The result is a uniform coat color.

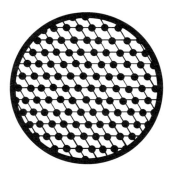

STANDARD BAY: *Quarter Horse*

29

BLOOD BAY

BLOOD BAY IS A VERY EYE-CATCHING SHADE, and to a horse fancier it is the most attractive of the different shades of bay. However, laboratory research and practical use show that blood bay is more susceptible to damage by heat, sweat and pressure than any of the other shades of bay. The reason for this is that there are channels in the hair, completely devoid of pigmentation, which allow a greater quantity of light to pass through. The refraction of light through the pigment gives the reddish, lustrous cast of the blood bay as shown in the painting.

A cross section shows clear spaces between "panels" of pigment deposits which run the length of the hair and increase the intake of light.

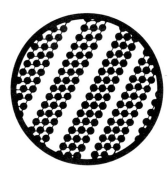

BLOOD BAY: *Quarter Horse*

31

LIGHT BAY

LIGHT BAY, for all general purposes, has a hide sufficiently dark enough to withstand all that is required of any color, but the lack of density of pigment in the shaft of the hair, as shown by the drawing, fails to give it as much resistance to sunlight and heat as the other described shades of bay.

Fewer pigment deposits absorb less light, allowing greater refraction and resulting in the lightest of the bay colors.

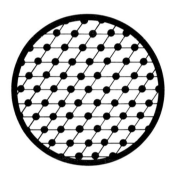

LIGHT BAY: *Arabian*

33

BROWN

THE BEST KNOWN and most clearly defined shades of brown are standard brown and seal brown. A horse with brown hair has a very durable hide. Standard brown and its lesser shades are subject to the "sunburn" appearance, caused by the process where sweat enters into fine cracks in the hair, that is found in the other intense colors, black and dark bay.

STANDARD BROWN

THE PATTERN OF PIGMENTATION in the shaft of the hair that produces standard brown, as illustrated, affords no open passageway through the shaft of the hair in a straight course. By studying the pigment pattern you can see that in standard brown light is deflected as well as refracted, and the variance of this could cause several different shades of brown.

A diagram of the hair sliced lengthwise shows the solid rows of pigment deposits with open passages around them.

STANDARD BROWN: *Morgan*

37

SEAL BROWN

THE PIGMENT PATTERN of seal brown is spaced and arranged in a way that the ends of the rows of pigment barely overlap, and light is more greatly refracted than reflected. This creates the reddish cast to the brown pattern and is referred to as seal brown.

Occasional gaps in the rows of pigment deposits change the refraction of light in a way that gives a reddish cast to the color.

SEAL BROWN: *Morgan*

39

BLACK

THE PIGMENT IN THE HAIR of black horses is dense and compact in the shaft of the hair, and no light passes through the hair. In the absence of any refraction of light, black is the only color. The shaft of the hair on a coal black horse is not as smooth as that on a raven black horse and is inclined to have a dull finish. Coal black, in general, belongs to the draft and heavy-boned breeds and the cobby type of pony breeds. Raven black is generally thought of as belonging to the light-boned breeds of horses — Thoroughbreds, Arabians, American Saddle Horses and others.

COAL BLACK

IN COAL BLACK HORSES the pigment is laid exactly perpendicular to the shaft of the hair and picks up no reflection of light. Any sheen that may show on the hair will be a clear sheen caused by the oils of the skin of a well-groomed, coal black horse.

The diagram shows the arrangement of pigment deposits perpendicular to the shaft of the hair allowing no passage of light.

COAL BLACK: *Percheron*

43

RAVEN BLACK

IN RAVEN BLACK the pigment is extremely compact in the hair, and the layers are laid in stacks perpendicular to the outside shaft of the hair. The additional sheen picked up by the raven black is caused by the pigment being at a slight angle, and the very edges pick up sufficient light to cause the reflection of purplish sheen highlights.

*The angled pigment pattern causes
a little more reflection of highlights
because of the angulation.*

RAVEN BLACK: *American Saddle Horse*

45

GREY

THE COLOR GREY in horses has long been one of the most controversial colors in the opinions of horsemen. There are equally as many who love the color grey as there are those who despise it. The greatest objection to grey among all horsemen is that it continues to get lighter with age, and by the time a horse is ten or twelve years old, it has generally lost the darkness in its body color. By then it has only some dappled and mixed grey color in its hindquarters, forequarters, all four legs and possibly a little under the throat and the lower part of the belly.

Most all grey horses are born black with little or no white hair in their coats. As they begin to shed their baby hair around their heads, feet and legs, their yearling hair begins to form the coat. The first very faint scattering of white hair will be noticed around their ears and eyes, and then still later there will be a very few white hairs show up in their coats, scattered along the backs and rumps. In general appearance they are still black, and it takes close examination to find the first white hairs.

When this animal sheds as a two-year-old, there will be much more white hair all over the coat, and the head will begin to have a dark grey appearance. The coat becomes lighter each year with white hair gradually replacing black hair. There is actually no grey hair on a grey horse. The color grey is created by white and black hairs that grow from a black hide.

Two- and three-year-old horses are ofttimes referred to as steel grey because the white hair is in much lesser quantity than the black hair. Four- to seven-year-olds will have a dappling grey pattern and are often referred to as dapple blue or blue-grey because the white and black hairs are so near the same quantity that the horse will have a blue-grey look. Eight- and nine-year-olds are actually dappled grey because the white hair has reached a much higher percentage of his overall body coat. The overall color continues to lighten through the next several years until the horse is referred to as a "white" horse. This is improper in that he still has a black hide and slight grey markings around the joints of his legs and feet. He is never a true white, but a grey-white.

The color grey has been referred to down through the ages as being a symptom of a "diseased" hide. Writers as far back as 1300 A.D. describe the color grey as resulting from a "diseased" hide. This misconception has been repeated and accepted without investigation from a scientific point of view all the way down to modern times. Diseases are caused by many forms of infection and are not hereditary; therefore, this cannot be true. Body conditions are hereditary, and a body condition that would cause animal life to be susceptible to certain diseases could be hereditary. The word disease has been misused, improperly applied and wrongly

---

ILLUSTRATION A. *All hairs are filled with pigment in the hide of an unborn grey foal, and thus he is born black.*

ILLUSTRATION B. *By the time the horse is three years old, the first layer of pigment-producing tissue has gone dry. The hairs rooted there turn white.*

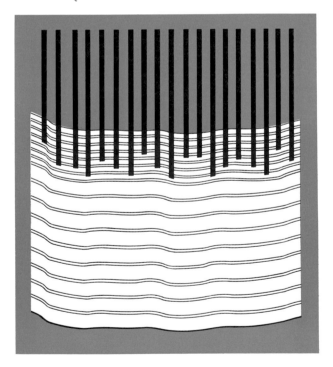
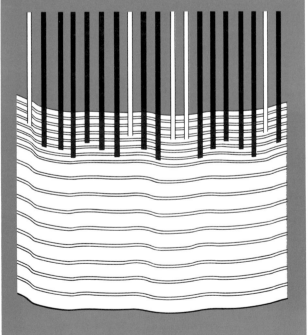

48

translated by all writers on the color grey to the present time. The hide of a grey horse is deficient only in its production of pigment, which is far from being a disease.

Pigment is in abundance in all pigment layers in the tender hide of the unborn foal. All hair is not rooted to the same depth, but as the hair grows on the unborn foal, even the most shallow-rooted hair is rooted in an abundance of pigment which accounts for the grey foal being born black. See illustration A.

The first pigment layers of a grey horse produce a lesser amount of pigment even before this foal is a year old. The most shallow-rooted hair is around the eyes and ears, and it is the first hair that will eventually lose its color. Thereafter, the greying process begins.

ILLUSTRATION C. *By age seven, the second layer of pigment-producing tissue has gone dry, resulting in more white hairs, and a dappled appearance.*

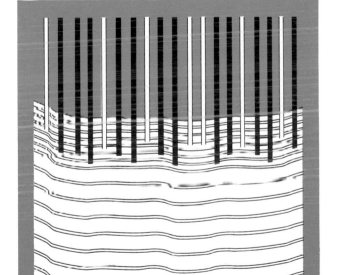

ILLUSTRATION D. *The process continues until the horse is light grey at eight years of age and nearly white by the time he is ten years old.*

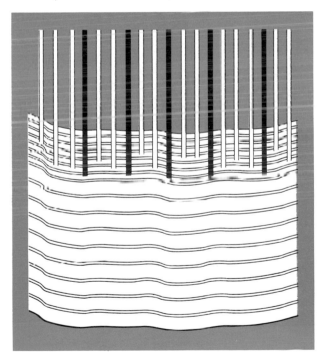

49

As the foal develops into a yearling, the three layers of upper dermis tissue do not contain pigment that can impart color in the hair, and it is in the fourth layer of dermis tissue where the first pigment is available. When the pigment-producing glands of the first pigment layer begin to fail in production, the hair rooted to the first pigment layer turns white because there is no pigment to be "picked up." Illustration B shows that little or no pigment is left in the first pigment layer, and the hair that was rooted to the first layer has turned white.

In illustration C we are looking at the hair and hide of a seven-year-old and we can see that the same process occurs except that another pigment layer has ceased to produce pigment; therefore, more white hairs appear.

ILLUSTRATION E.

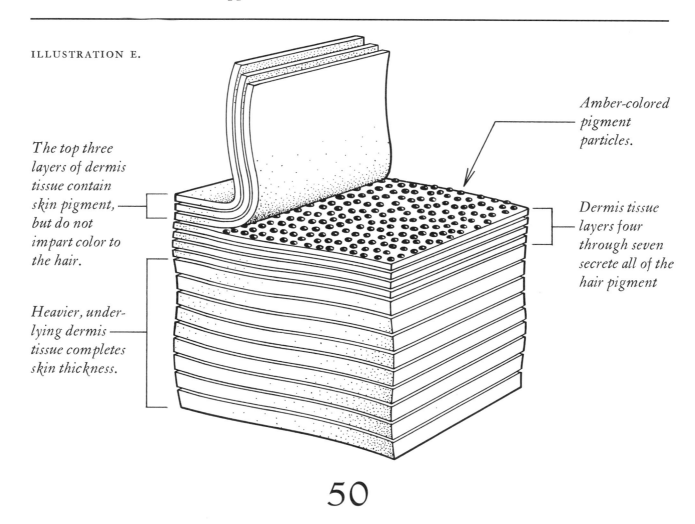

The top three layers of dermis tissue contain skin pigment, but do not impart color to the hair.

Heavier, underlying dermis tissue completes skin thickness.

Amber-colored pigment particles.

Dermis tissue layers four through seven secrete all of the hair pigment

50

Eight-year-olds that are continuing to lose pigment are growing lighter, and all the available pigment then is at the fourth pigment layer, which is the seventh dermis layer. Since this fourth pigment layer is the deepest of those producing pigment, it has been the least affected by the toughening process which affects the outer layers of the hide. Thus the pigment glands survive to produce pigment after those above it have quit producing. All horses eight years and older must pick up pigment from the seventh layer, which is the last pigment layer, as shown in illustration D. Often there continues to be a small supply of pigment in the hide of the hair over the knees, hocks and ankles, which are the last points on a grey horse that finally turn grey-white.

This aging and toughening process of the hide of a grey horse causes the pigment to recede. Therefore the pigment glands of that layer cease to function until in a ten- to twelve-year-old there is very little pigment available in the hide covering the upper part of the horse's body. As the fluid content of the pigment layers recede, the grey horse finally develops the toughest hide of any horse whatever his color.

In illustration E the three top dermis tissues are laid back and the drawing shows the tiny specks of pigment available on the top of the fourth dermis layer, the first pigment layer, which are in a dew-like pattern.

GREY TWO-YEAR-OLD

WHEN A GREY HORSE is two years old, the first layers of the pigment glands begin to fail and white hairs appear in the overall body coat.

The two-year-old grey has continued to lose more pigment. It is therefore lighter than the yearling whose hair is shown in illustration B on page 48.

GREY—TWO-YEAR-OLD: *Thoroughbred*

53

GREY THREE- TO FOUR-YEAR-OLD

DURING THE THIRD and fourth years of the life of a grey horse, there is the continued failure of the second layer, and the beginning failure of the third layer of the pigment glands, giving the steel grey color that gradually approaches dappling.

This horse is lighter still than the two-year-old. It has more hairs which have lost their pigment and is a further development of the hair pattern shown for the yearling in illustration B on page 48.

54

GREY—three- to four-year-old: *Arabian*

55

GREY FOUR- TO SEVEN-YEAR-OLD

THE CONTINUING FAILURE of the layers of pigment glands in four- through seven-year-old greys produces a color described as dapple-blue or blue-grey.

Dappling is fully apparent in a horse this age. See illustration C on page 49.

GREY—FOUR- TO SEVEN-YEAR-OLD: *Quarter Horse*

57

GREY TEN YEARS AND OLDER

WHEN A GREY HORSE is ten years and older, failure of the pigment pattern continues until the pigment glands have ceased to function from the third through the seventh layers. He is then grey-white except in the hide over the knees, hocks and ankles, which are the last points on a grey horse to turn grey-white.

By the time a grey reaches this age he has lost almost all pigment in all hair. See illustration D on page 49.

GREY—TEN YEARS AND OLDER: *Percheron*

59

DUN

DUN IS A COLOR that has always been found among horses in a wild state, and the early wild horses of Northwestern America had many dun animals among them. Dun is rarely ever found in horses that have been bred for racing and show purposes, except in quarter horses. The quarter horse, of course, derives much of his background from native-bred horses.

The color dun can be easily observed as having black points, black mane and tail and often-times has black zebra-like stripes above its knee and hock. The dark stripe over the shoulder belongs to the dun as well as the black stripe down the spine from the mane to the tail.

The pigment pattern in the body hair of a dun horse has the peculiarity of a dense pigment arrangement in the tip end of the hair. The shaft of the hair from the tip back towards the body has the uniform color of dun. When a dun horse turns its neck or moves in such a manner that would cause most colors to show a sheen, dun will show a smuttiness because the densely pigmented tip ends of the hair are brought so close together that they give a smutty appearance.

The hide of a dun horse is extremely durable, and dun hair has the characteristic of good light refraction. Little damage can be done to the hide and hair of a dun horse by heat, sweat and pressure. Varying shades of dun that may be seen among horses all carry the tough hide, and light refracting quality. Little or no serviceable difference can be pointed out in the lightest or darkest shades of dun.

A layer of pigment deposited on the bottom side of each hair terminates in a solidly pigmented tip end.

60

DUN: *Native-bred*

61

SELF COLORS

CHESTNUT

Liver Chestnut

Dark Chestnut

Standard Chestnut

Bright Chestnut

Dusty Chestnut

Light Chestnut

SORREL

Chestnut Sorrel

Dark Sorrel

Standard Sorrel

Bright Sorrel

Light Sorrel

Blond Sorrel

BUCKSKIN

COPPER DUN

SELF COLORS ARE RECESSIVE to all of the intense colors. Being recessive to an intense color, it is the general rule that self-colors bred back to each other will not produce intense colors. The lighter shades of self colors, when bred together, have a small percentage of fallout which is the origin of dilute colors.

All self colors have lost, to some degree, the ruggedness and resistance in the hair and hide of the intense colors from which they are derived.

CHESTNUT

IN RECENT TIMES horsemen have expressed concern about so many breeds and classes of horses "turning" chestnut. This trend towards chestnut could have been caused by several factors: 1. the selection of chestnuts because of their attractive color, and 2. many chestnuts are excellent performing horses by reason of their breeding, and are therefore more popular.

Chestnut is probably the best of the self colors, and it is recessive to all dominant colors. Horses with bloodlines and records of many generations of dominant colors can produce chestnut offspring. The darkest chestnut occasionally will have small spots of black in its coat, generally over the rump and along the back. None of these spots are very large, and they are never close together. The opposite extreme of this in chestnut is that sometimes the standard and lighter shades can have a mingling of white hairs that are not sufficient to qualify as roan. The darker self colors, selected and crossbred, in many cases will produce the same shade. Lighter chestnuts can come from intense colors, but it is through the usual breeding of darker shades of chestnut to chestnut that the lighter shades are produced.

Chestnuts also are the source of some shades of dilute colors, but in one study after breeding records were kept on some two thousand or more foals, an intense color was never reproduced.

Microscopically, chestnut pigment pattern has the appearance of a cloud-like arrangement of pigment bodies fused together in odd numbers from three through seven. There may be an even number of pigment particles in a chestnut cloud, but I have never found one. As in all other pigmentation of the hair, a very fine needle of pigment is thrown to the other cloud-like patterns, and these little needle-like particles stabilize the pattern in the shaft of the hair. They do not add or detract more than a very small percentage in the refraction of light in the pigment pattern itself. The density of these cloud-like patterns creates the darker shades of chestnut, and the less dense clouds account for lighter shades.

LIVER CHESTNUT

LIVER CHESTNUT IS the darkest shade of the self colors, and the hide of a liver chestnut withstands heat, light reflection and "sunburn" exceptionally well, though it is not as resistant as the first four shades of bay. There has been controversy as to whether the liver chestnut is an intense color or a self color. This confusion may result from the fact that the liver chestnut is the darkest shade of the self colors, the pigment in the shaft of the hair is the most intense of the self colors, and, as shown by the illustration, it has the densest pigmentation in the shaft of the hair of the self color patterns.

*Triangular-shaped clusters of pigment
deposits composed of five or seven particles
are arranged in a tight pattern that allows
the refraction of very little light
through the hair.*

LIVER CHESTNUT: *Standardbred*

69

DARK CHESTNUT

DARK CHESTNUT IS equally as serviceable a hide and hair as liver chestnut. The difference in the shade occurs because of the slight difference in pigment and the greater refraction of light.

All shades of chestnut will scald more under heat, pressure and sweat than those of intense colors. This is evidence that the cloud-like pattern of pigmentation in the shaft of the hair does not give as much protection to the hide as the denser patterns in the hair of the intense colors.

In all chestnut colors except the liver chestnut, the clusters of pigment deposits are composed of three or five particles. This color is lighter because the concentration of pigment is less intense.

70

DARK CHESTNUT: *Quarter Horse*

71

STANDARD CHESTNUT

STANDARD CHESTNUT HAS sufficient pigmentation in the hide and hair to be equally useful and is a uniform color all over the horse's body, with the only light tones being the highlights in the coat.

A lighter concentration of pigment clusters results in a uniform chestnut color.

STANDARD CHESTNUT: *Thoroughbred*

73

BRIGHT CHESTNUT

BRIGHT CHESTNUT IS the first shade of chestnut in which refraction of light is very brilliant to the eye, and is not as protective to the hide. It is the first shade of the self colors that would be subject to the caustic effects of sand-scald, not to be confused with "sunburn."

The diagram shows an even lighter concentration of pigment clusters.

BRIGHT CHESTNUT: *Thoroughbred*

75

DUSTY CHESTNUT

DUSTY CHESTNUT IS the most peculiar of the shades of chestnut. The pigmentation of the hide makes it generally as durable as the standard chestnut. The hair has the peculiar quality of having the tip ends fused together and solid; consequently, the pigmentation cannot be motivated by the electrons the full extent of the shaft of the hair. The overlying faint pigmentation of the ends of hair against the pigmented areas of the hair underneath gives the dusty appearance. However, the section of the shaft of the hair that is pigmented is of the chestnut cloud-like pattern, and a horse this color does not have a weak-pigmented hide.

The diagram shows the fused tip end of the hair which blocks the passage of pigment into that area.

DUSTY CHESTNUT: *Thoroughbred*

77

LIGHT CHESTNUT

LIGHT CHESTNUT IS a controversial color from the standpoint of classification. Breeding light chestnut back to the darker shades of chestnut and many of the intense colors quite often will throw darker chestnut offspring. However, there could be some argument as to whether it should be classified as a self color or a dilute color in view of the fact that two light chestnuts sometimes throw a dilute in skin pigment with hair color that is lighter than many shades of chestnut. That foal might be classified as claybank or occasionally palomino. So to definitely state that all chestnuts are self colors is questionable, especially when applied to light chestnut.

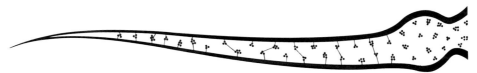

This is the lightest concentration of pigment in all the shades of chestnut.

LIGHT CHESTNUT: *Quarter Horse*

79

SORREL

SORREL HAS LESS PIGMENT in hair and hide than the other self colors and is usually considered to belong to the draft horse breeds. The hide of the draft breeds is thicker and can withstand more abuse than the thin hide of the light-boned chestnut breeds. However, this is not true of the color sorrel.

The pigmentation in all shades of sorrel is less than the comparable shades of chestnut. The three top layers of dermis tissue in sorrel do not contain as much pigment as other self colors and are more subject to the effects of sunrays, pressure and sweat. The lightest shades of sorrel do not have durable hides and must receive more attention in the fitting of harness and other trappings to prevent as much scuffing and chaffing as possible.

Sorrel horses sometimes have hooves as black as the intense colors, but for the most part their hooves are an amber color and require more care and shoeing than the darker-hooved horses. The manes and tails of chestnut sorrel, dark sorrel and standard sorrel should be the same shade as the rest of the horse's coat to be true representatives of their shade, whereas, the remaining lighter shades must all have flaxen manes and tails to be true representatives of their shades. All shades of sorrel have a lighter shade of hair on their lower legs from the knees and hocks to the ground. The pigment bodies in sorrel are deposited in a circular formation inside the wall of the hair. The number of circles of pigment determine how light or dark the sorrel may be. However, there is never any pigment in a circle in the exact center of the hair. When the refraction of light passes through the pigment bodies and strikes the non-pigmented center, it creates a glow that causes the buff tone to show through. This explains why the undertone of all sorrels has a light cast to it and the hair on the legs becomes lighter from the body to the hoof, whereas, chestnut horses' legs become darker than their top coat from the knees and hocks to the ground.

CHESTNUT SORREL

CHESTNUT SORREL, as confusing as this description of shade may sound, has long been the way to describe the darkest shade of sorrel. The horse of this dark shade should have a mane and tail of matching color, and to be a true sorrel, the hair on the legs from the knee joints and hocks to the feet will be of a much lighter shade, which portrays the buffing effect of the pigment pattern. The chestnut sorrel has the most durable hide among the sorrel shades.

The cross section shows heavy pigment deposits around the outside wall of the hair. The small opening in the center runs the entire length of the hair.

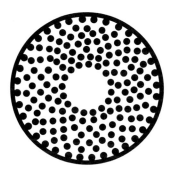

CHESTNUT SORREL: *Belgian*

83

DARK SORREL

DARK SORREL IS DARK, as the name implies, with the lower body and the underbelly being considerably lighter than chestnut sorrel and with more buff showing in the hair on the lower legs down to the hoof. Dark sorrel has a serviceable hide and in some instances may have black hooves. However, this shade usually begins to show a dark amber pigmentation in the hoof.

The pigment layer inside the wall of the hair is thinner than that of the chestnut sorrel, and the center opening, consequently, is wider.

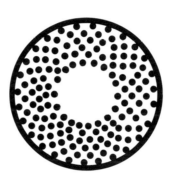

DARK SORREL: *Belgian*

85

STANDARD SORREL

STANDARD SORREL IS uniformly the same color all over the body with the legs from the middle joints down to the hoof being of a still lighter shade. The mane and tail can be a shade lighter than the overall body color. This is caused by an intermingling of lighter hair with hair of the body color.

In this and in succeeding lighter shades of sorrel the layers of pigment become lesser and the central opening wider.

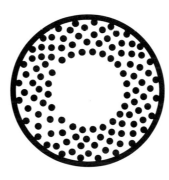

STANDARD SORREL: *Belgian*

87

BRIGHT SORREL

BRIGHT SORREL HAS a lesser pigment pattern and has the appearance of a glow. The leg coloring from the middle joints down is considerably lighter, and the horse should have a flaxen mane and tail to be a true representative of the shade. The hide of this color has lost some durability when compared to the darker shades.

In this hair more than two-thirds of the center of the shaft is open, and the pigment layer is thinner than that of the standard sorrel.

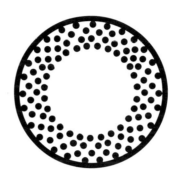

BRIGHT SORREL: *Belgian*

89

LIGHT SORREL

LIGHT SORREL IS a uniform color with flaxen mane and tail, but does not possess the glow of bright sorrel because of the difference in the quantity of the pigment which causes a lesser refraction of light. The hide of light sorrel is slightly more durable than bright sorrel, but it does not possess the durability of the darker shades.

Again the open central core of the hair shaft has grown larger, and the pigment layer which circles the inside layer of the shaft is reduced to an extremely thin layer just inside the shaft walls.

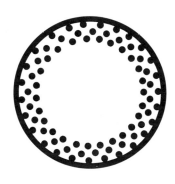

LIGHT SORREL: *Belgian*

91

BLOND SORREL

BLOND SORREL MUST have a flaxen mane and tail, the lighter the better. The upper regions of the body should have slight sorrel coloring with the shoulders and underbelly being much lighter. However, as little pigment as there is in the hair, it is still of the sorrel pattern and is not to be confused with palomino. The blond sorrel coloring continues down the legs to the hoofs in its lighter pattern, and it would be hoped that there is still sufficient pigment in the hoof to impart a slight amber color. The hide of this color requires much more attention when fitting harness and trappings to prevent chaffing, scald and other hair and skin impairments.

Blond sorrel is verging on a dilute, and when blond individuals are bred to each other a high percentage of the offspring will be dilute.

This is the lightest shade of sorrel. It has the thinnest layer of pigment and the largest center opening.

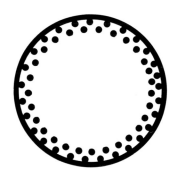

BLOND SORREL: *Belgian*

93

BUCKSKIN

THE BODY COLOR buckskin is a self color and is clean of any of the smuttiness that might appear in other colors. As the name implies, a true-colored buckskin horse with black points that do not extend above the knees should be the color of a tanned deerhide.

A black mane and tail is characteristic of the color. However, the guard hairs growing off of the coat and up over the base of the mane and tail should be a clean, clear buckskin color fringing the black mane and tail at the body.

The color is a durable one, and usually the feet are black. Unless there is an unusual amount of white markings in the face, the eyes range in color from a very dark amber shading to black.

A buckskin horse sometimes has a black stripe down the spine from the mane to the root of the tail.

The pigment deposits are arranged very much like those of a dun, but the buckskin has no concentration of pigment at the tip ends of the hair.

BUCKSKIN: *Quarter Horse*

95

COPPER DUN

COPPER DUN IS a self color and the pigment pattern within the shaft of the hair might be considered a confusing pattern in that it is a double color. The chestnut color of the markings on the legs from the knees and hocks to the ground and the chestnut color of the mane and tail and the stripe down the spine have the cloud-like true chestnut pattern. The overall body color is neither chestnut nor dun. However, the overlapping pigment pattern in the shaft of the hair and the general markings and color of the copper dun make it a self color. The pigment pattern in the shaft of the hair which makes up the overall body color is the same overlapping pattern as the intense color, dun, but its lesser density and refraction and absorption of a greater amount of light make copper dun a self color rather than an intense color.

The hide of a copper dun horse is comparable in serviceable qualities to that of a standard chestnut. It withstands heat and light equally as well, but tends to have less durability and resistance to pressure. The hooves can be black, however, in most instances the hoof is generally a dark amber color and, when devoid of white markings, is still a serviceable hoof.

The pigment is deposited in a distinctive pattern that allows more refraction of light. This pigment arrangement over the body is similar to dun. However, the lower part of the legs and mane and tail are of the chestnut pattern.

COPPER DUN: *Quarter Horse*

97

OTHER COLORS

ROAN

Red Roan

Blue Roan

Rose Grey

GRULLA

OTHER COLORS is a designation used to describe the horses of useful hair and hide patterns that are not definable in the previous color classifications. They have peculiarities in the pigment pattern arrangements of the hair or an absence of such pigment which results in parti-colored horses.

ROAN

THE COLOR ROAN is produced by the intermingling of a base color with white hairs through-out the coat. There is actually no roan hair, i.e., a hair with mixed color. The white hair in the roaning pattern is far different from a base color hair in that it is a solid hair with no shaft opening in the center of it. It is not caused by an absence of pigment in the hide. But, even though there is pigment in the hide, it has no means of migrating up through the shaft of the hair. This pattern of coloring does not grow lighter or darker because of age. It is not caused by the receding of pigmentation, as is true in the grey horse; nor is it the absence of pigmentation such as in white markings or albinos.

Roan horses can be described by their base color such as bay roan, red roan and so forth. Base color, as referred to in roans, means any solid color exclusive of white hair. The only shade that differs is blue roan in which the base color is black, and the intermingling of white hair gives a blue appearance.

All roan horses, regardless of shade, will have solid-colored heads, and the legs from the knee joints and hock joints to the hoof will be the same base color as the head. The manes and tails will usually be colors which correspond to the base color. However, although it is not the usual pattern, they are sometimes the same roan color.

RED ROAN

A CHESTNUT BASE intermingled with the solid-shaft, white hair that causes the roaning pattern is known as red roan. The head and legs from the knees and hocks to the hoof are chestnut colored. The mane and tail generally are the same true base color. However, an intermingling of the white roaning hair with the base color in the mane and tail is not uncommon.

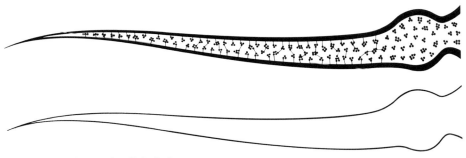

Intermingling of solid shaft
white hairs with chestnut hairs results
in the red roan color.

RED ROAN: *Standardbred*

105

BLUE ROAN

THE SAME DESCRIPTION applies to blue roan as red roan, with the exception being the base color, which in this case, is always black.

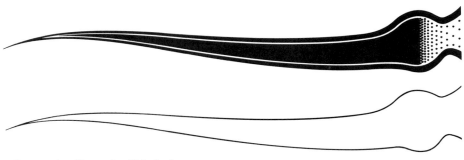

Intermingling of solid shaft white hairs with black hairs results in the blue roan color.

BLUE ROAN: *Tennessee Walker*

107

ROSE GREY

ROSE GREY IS classified by itself and is in fact a roan. This is not a true grey and should not be described as such since its color is stable throughout the horse's lifetime. There can be various shades of chestnut base color, and the only distinguishing difference in rose grey and red roan is that the entire coat is of the same mixed color. The roaning pattern should continue in the head and downward through the legs to the hoof. The mane and tail should also carry the roaning factor in a shade comparable to the rest of the animal's body. The durability of the hide of a rose grey is dependent on the base color of chestnut that the roaning pattern is blended with. Arabian breeders are the only ones that classify the color to be rose grey.

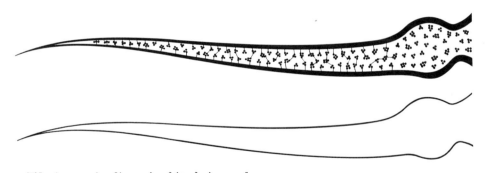

The intermingling of white hairs and chestnut hairs extends over the entire coat.

ROSE GREY: *Arabian*

109

GRULLA

GRULLA IS CONSIDERED an intense color. However, due to the pigment arrangement in the shaft of the hair, there is some room for question. Grulla is sometimes described as blue or dove or mouse-colored. The blue grulla is actually the only horse that could be described as light blue or soft grey.

The pigment pattern of grulla is somewhat complex as you will observe from the illustration. The pigment leaves the follicle in an intense fine line that migrates up through the center the full length of the shaft of the hair. Pigment then is sent from this line to the outside shaft of the hair in partition-like formations that cause a thin curtain-like pattern allowing the light to come through the shaft of the hair directly to the intense pigment core. However, light is not refracted completely from one wall to the other wall of the shaft, and the reflection back from the so-called partition creates the haziness within the shaft of the hair that is perceived optically as light blue or soft grey. The hide of the grulla horse is comparable in durability to the intense colors, is well-pigmented and can withstand extreme heat, pressure and sunlight. The refraction pattern in the shaft of the hair is seldom ever affected by sweat and heat. The feet are heavily pigmented, usually thick-walled and can withstand rocks and hard use.

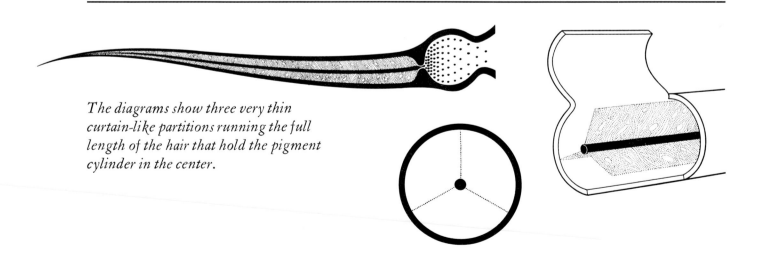

The diagrams show three very thin curtain-like partitions running the full length of the hair that hold the pigment cylinder in the center.

GRULLA: *Quarter Horse*

111

DILUTES

PALOMINO

CLAYBANK

DILUTES ARE UNDESIRABLE COLORS in a horse intended for useful purposes. The pigment-producing glands are far less active and produce so little pigment that the three top layers of the hide do not have sufficient pigmentation to be properly resistant to heat, sunlight and pressure. The lack of pigment in the hide keeps the hair from picking up enough pigment for the production of a good useful color. This is further affected by the fact that the opening of the follicle going into the shaft of the hair on dilute colors is so small that what pigment is available cannot enter into the shaft of the hair in a pattern dense enough to properly protect the already deficiently pigmented hide. Pigmentation continues to diminish when dilutes are continuously bred to each other, and the hide of each generation will be less durable and useful until, in a few generations, it finally becomes albino.

PALOMINO

PALOMINO, AS DESCRIBED by the registries that have been established for the color (palomino is not a breed), say that palomino should be the color of twenty-two carat gold. Much discussion could arise from the difference, if any, in the appearance of ten, fourteen, eighteen or twenty-two carat gold. For this reason palomino is being described as a golden color.

The pigment pattern that refracts light to reflect the gold color of palomino is the result of the way that pigment is expelled outward through the shaft of the hair from the follicle. The opening of the follicle in a palomino hair is so small that the pigment, propelled by its electrons, is pushed through such a small opening that it enters the shaft of the hair in a "smear" rather than a full-bodied spherically-shaped deposit. This "smear" coating the inside of the shaft of the hair is so thinly spread that the refraction of light gives off the golden palomino color.

The hide of the palomino horse is lightly pigmented and useful, but not nearly as durable as the self and intense colors. The hooves are generally an amber color with insufficient pigment and are more susceptible to brittleness and are subject to cracking. The color palomino is not inclined to sunburn. However, the hide will not stand an extreme amount of heat or pressure, and this color horse is never found in the sand-scalding regions of the world.

The horses with the purest palomino color always have manes and tails that are lighter than their body color, but seldom "pure" white.

The constricted opening between the follicle and the shaft of the hair severely impedes the flow of pigment. The "smeared" pigment deposits, indicated by the dotted line, form a coating on the inside wall of the hair.

PALOMINO: *Quarter Horse*

117

CLAYBANK

CLAYBANK IS THE DILUTE of the color copper dun. The slanted pattern of the pigmentation in the body color of claybank is the same pattern as that of copper dun. The difference in the lighter-shaded claybank is caused by a lesser amount of pigmentation in each pigment line, and a greater distance between the lines which provide room for the entrance of more light.

The hide of a claybank horse is not durable when exposed to really hard use, and the lack of density in the hide causes it to be more sensitive to heat and pressure. This pattern is not subject to sunburn, however, because it does not absorb much light. The color of the eye of a claybank is amber, and the darker the better. The hooves of horses of this color generally are lightly-pigmented and border on brittleness.

The diagram shows a similarity to the pigment pattern of the copper dun. The claybank has less pigment in the pattern extending through the shaft of the hair.

CLAYBANK: *Quarter Horse*

119

MARKINGS

ALL COLORS and all breeds of horses are subject to having white markings on their feet, legs and heads. Various horse registries have information available to their breeders regarding markings, and furnish diagrams showing the exact position and description of each marking, such as the class of sock, e.g., half sock, full sock. Head markings are described as star and stripe, bald face, snip and so forth.

The white markings on a horse serve the purpose of identification. In view of the fact that there are many sources of information available on markings, this text does not propose to set a standard of markings that would be in agreement or conflict with those already preferred by horse organizations.

SPOTS, PAINTS, PINTOS, PIEBALDS, AND APPALOOSAS

REGARDLESS OF THE PATTERN of dark and white hide that covers a horse's body—call it spots, paint, pinto, piebald or appaloosa—no breed can be established on color. All the horse registries in the world that have survived the test of time and have been of service to mankind have recorded horses that were bred for a type that would serve a specific purpose. A horse is bred for muscle structure, and in part, bone structure, to perform a certain feat or a useful purpose to mankind, whether it be a Thoroughbred for racing, a standardbred for light harness or the draft breed for hard pulling and so forth. To try to establish a breed by color is one of the fallacies of the thinking of so-called horsemen.

Parti colored horses have hides with areas that are non-pigmented, which creates white. The darker area of the hide which contains pigment is some shade of color. A horse that does not have a durable hide cannot withstand harness, saddles and other trappings of man and would be useless as a beast of burden. The darker-colored hide of a horse would be the most useful since it is the pigment which is contained in the colored hide that gives the hide the ability to withstand heat, pressure and the rubbing and chaffing of harness and saddles. The white hide on a horse is much thinner because of the absence of pigment and is subject to scalding, blistering and peeling.

White hide around the eyes does not deflect sunlight, and the eyes are more apt to be sore from the absorption of light. A horse with such eyes will be less useful. A dark eye contains phosphorous pigment that enables a horse to catch the slightest glimmer of light and see in the night. On a non-pigmented white-faced horse, the eyeball and the inner area of the eye have no pigment, or at least have little pigment, and the horse is generally referred to as being glass-eyed or marble-eyed. This absence of color in the eye causes the horse not to have all of the reflective quality that enables a horse to see and severely affects his vision, especially at night.

The white foot of a horse does not hold the natural oils of the hoof which normally prevent the hoof from cracking. Also, the walls of a white hoof are soft and wear and break more easily from rough terrain than those of a dark-colored hoof. The appearance of spots, paints, pintos, piebalds and appaloosas is pleasing to the unknowing eye, but there is no practical reason for mankind to have ever endeavored to weaken the useful purpose of the horse by breeding out pigments essential for soundness and deflection of light.

A NOTE ON THE PAINTINGS

THROUGHOUT HISTORY people have made attempts to identify the color of horses. None of them have been particularly successful. However, once the colors were described, the problem became how to reproduce those colors in some manner so that horse people whether in Europe or New England or the American Southwest or elsewhere throughout the world would have a standard reference to use in identifying horse color.

In preparing this book, consideration was given to using exact color photographs of horses to depict the various colors, but the difficulties were enormous. First was the matter of trying to find thirty-four horses with perfect color, good conformation, and in the right mix of breeds. And on top of that were the technical and logistical difficulties encountered in attempting to photograph them with standardized, controlled lighting and backgrounds.

The solution to this myriad of problems was to find an artist who knew horse anatomy and who could paint well. We found him in Darol Dickinson.

Then for a period of more than two years the author, Dr. Ben Green, worked closely with Dickinson. Dr. Green gave the talented young artist explicit information on the specific colors, tones, shading and markings to be used on each horse. Dr. Green also specified which breed and conformation characteristics each horse should have.

Every finished painting was approved by Dr. Green as matching his descriptions which are based on the scientific research which he began three decades ago.

Then a full-color printed proof of each oil painting was submitted to the author for final approval as matching his findings and the artist's paintings.

The thirty-four paintings are now maintained together as a permanent collection and will be displayed throughout the country.

THE EDITOR